DEAR YOUNGER ME

Dear Younger Me

A Reflection in Poetry

LINDSAY GORDON

Lines By Linds

First Printing, 2024

Dedicated to six of the most beautiful blessings in my life,
my nieces and nephews:
Calvin, Eleanor, Ryan, Blake, Lorelai, and Sierra.

I love you all so much, my heart could just explode.
I'm with you all, till the end of the line.

Preface

The older I get, the more reflective I become. This has become especially true once I became an aunt. My life was changed forever when my first nephew, Calvin, was born. Over time, our family grew to give me six nieces and nephews. Being an aunt is one of my absolute favorite things that I get to be in this life; I never knew my heart could hold so much love until I held Calvin for the first time, and even more so when I met every niece and nephew who came after. But since becoming an aunt, and since working in fields that surround me with a lot of young people, I find myself in reflective states more frequently, thinking back to who I was when I was younger. What would I tell myself if I could? What would I have done differently? What do I wish I had known? What wisdom could I possibly share with my past self, or maybe more helpfully, with the next generation?

Dear Younger Me serves a dual purpose – addressing my inner child (and maybe experiencing some personal healing in the process), while also sharing the wisdom and lessons I've learned, keeping my six favorite people in mind. This book is me answering the question, "What do I want to pass on to them?" So – Calvin, Eleanor, Ryan, Blake, Lorelai, and Sierra – this is my gift to you, a piece of me that will outlive me. And dear reader, I hope that it resonates with you, too.

DEAR YOUNGER ME

Why is it
that we
often don't
recognize
the sweetest
moments in life
until they are
long
past?

Be thankful
that you
didn’t
peak in
high school.

-but really though

Things actually
do
work out
better
than you
think
they will.

Comparing yourself
to others
will only
lead you to
Despair.
You're doing
fine –

I promise.

Timelines are
arbitrary.
Rules are
made up.
Just be
kind, and
do your
best.

Never take your
family –
parents,
aunts, uncles,
cousins,
grandparents,
great-grandparents –
for granted.

What I wouldn't
give
for just one
more day
with the ones I've
lost.

-i miss you

Having a
beautiful heart
will always be
more
valuable
than having a
pretty face.

-you're already beautiful

No
is your most
powerful
weapon.

Use it
wisely.

-mean it

Your mind
is a
powerful gift.
Feed it,
fuel it,
protect it,
and you will be
unstoppable.

Nurture
friendships that will
last a
lifetime.
The ones who stay with you
through it all
are
irreplaceable.

Romantic interests
will change
like the
wind.
Focus on building
foundational
friendships.
Strengthen your
circle.
Older you
will thank you.

You won't know
when you're taking
your last
neighborhood walk
or when everyone
is gathering at the
park for the
last time.

Cherish it
all.

People will
criticize you
no matter what.
As long as you
do what you
can with what
you have,
their remarks
are a
reflection on
them, not
on you.

School dances
are much more
fun
and much less
awkward
with friends
than with
a date.

Skip the
drama.

You do not
need to feel
guilty
for taking
care of
yourself.

Cars don't feel
guilty
when they need
gas.

You're never
too young
to start making
wise financial decisions
for your future
self.

Not every brain
works exactly
the same –
and that is
a good thing.

Your parents are
human beings.
They aren't
perfect.
They deserve grace,
too.

Being cherished
by the
right one
will make you
forget
the sting of
rejection
from all the
wrong ones
of the past.

-worth the wait

Being yourself
may not make you
popular
when you are
young,
but it will earn you
respect
as you
grow.

You don't
have to
carry it all
on your
own.

Asking for
help
is not
weak.

Not everyone
will like you
and that is
okay.

You won't
like everyone
either,

and that is
okay.

-just be kind

Stand up for
yourself
even if your
voice
shakes.
Be your own
strongest
ally.

If you want
someone to
depend on,

be
dependable.

Learn how to
fail
gracefully.

It will
happen,
but it does
not
have to
break you.

The longest
relationship
of your
life
is with
your body.
Take care
of it.

It will either
be your
friend, or your
enemy.

Always be
kind.
Everyone is
carrying their own
hardships.

Lead with
kindness.

Make them
work to
prove
their worth.
You are
precious –
don't give
yourself
away
too easily.

-you are worth it
-but they might not be

Understanding that
you will be
learning
for the
rest of your
life is not a
curse,
but rather a
gift.

You will
never
know it all, so
there is always
something
new to
learn.

-gift that keeps on giving

Take care
of the
world
around you.
God created
so much
beauty to
explore.
Protect it, and
experience it.

Learn to
enjoy
your own
company.
Go to the
theater
by yourself.
Have a meal
alone.
Be
content in
solitude.

-independence is bliss

Be inquisitive.
Ask insightful
questions
of the people
around you.
There is much
wisdom to be
earned
if you take the
time to
look for it.

-seek it like silver

Make art
even if it isn't
"good."

You don't
have to be
"good"
at something
for it to
bring you
joy.

Cry.

Let it out.

Don't be
ashamed of
your tears.
Tears mean
healing.
Let yourself
cry
without feeling
ashamed.

Don't try to
rush
growing up.
One day, you'll
miss the
times when you
had less to
worry about.

-be free

Try new things
even if they
scare you.
That is the
best way to
grow.

Help people
without
expecting
anything
in return.

Assume the
best in people
until proven
otherwise.
People are
generally
good, and
assuming the
worst
gets you
nowhere.

There is
magic
in this world.

It's called

love.

Enjoy your
youth.
Travel, eat,
spend time with
good people.
Life moves
fast,
with or
without you.

You are
more loved
than you could
ever know,
more precious
than you
realize,
more worthy
than you
understand.
Try to
hear it,
even if you
don't believe it
today.

You can
look ahead to
brighter days
without ignoring the
beauty
in the
stars.

Real friends will
tell you
when you are
wrong.

Be humble enough
to hear it.

Sweet child,
smile at your
reflection
for as long as you
can.

Time makes us
cruel
to ourselves.

Find the
one
who believes
you can do the
impossible
on the
days when
you can't
pull yourself
up off the
floor.

The world will
try to
teach you to
dread getting
older.

For as long as
possible,
try to view
each passing
year as an
opportunity –
for adventure,
for growth,
for enlightenment.

Hang on to that
childlike
wonder,
aglow with the
light of
candles on a
cake.

-happy birthday, eleanor

Cling
to the
encouraging words
of others –
try to let the
hurtful words
go.

Not all
souvenirs
from life are
physical, but
hold fast to them
anyway –
the sound of
his laughter,
the smell of her
perfume,
the staple
snacks of
get-togethers –
one day,
that will be
all you
have left of
them.

-hostess fruit pies

Keeping the
peace
matters –
but so does
keeping
your
peace.

-know the difference

Hold tightly
to the people that
make your
heart
smile.

Often, the
kindest people
have known the
deepest pain.

Listen to
understand
more readily
than you listen to
respond.

-two ears, one mouth

True love
is worth the
wait.
Don't rush or
settle.
Enjoy life with
yourself,
and love will
happen when the
time is
right.

You can
hold boundaries
firmly
and love people
at the
same time.

Commitment
means staying
true to your
word, even
if your
mood has
changed
since giving it.

Sometimes
truth is
painful –
but pain is
necessary for
growth.

The people
you can
learn
the most from
often do not
look
like you.

Speak
the same way
you would
saw lumber –
measure twice,
cut once.

-think before

Everyone
has a
story to tell.

It's harder to
hate someone
once you
know what they've
been through.

Are you
ready
to listen?

-listen to understand
-listen to love

Only say
yes
if you
actually
mean it.

Get your
hands
dirty –
make something,
create art,
plant seeds
and get in
touch
with the
earth.

-learn by doing

Never
assume that you
know
exactly who
will
show up for
you.

You may be
surprised
by who
doesn't –

but you may be
surprised by who
does.

I don’t think
you’ll ever
fully
understand just how
much your
family
couldn’t wait
to meet
you.

Each person who
loves you
has their
own
special
way
of showing up
for you.

Seek to
understand and
appreciate
each unique
way.

-countless ways to be loved

Real friends will
rejoice
with you in
your victories
even if they are
their
loss.

Stick with the
things that
bring you
joy, and
share them –

your joy will
double.

Battered and
bruised
is not the
same as
damaged and
used.

Your scars
do not
define
your
worth.

Losing their
trust
temporarily
instead of
losing them
forever
was worth it.

If you know
something is
wrong,

speak up.

Trust in God's
timing –
He will never
seem early,
but He will
never
be late.

Starting
therapy is
scary, but
unhealed
wounds are far
scarier.

Please be
kind
to yourself.

In the
blink
of an
eye,
everything
will change.

Time is a
thief.

Don't be
ashamed if you
can't find the
words
right away.

We all have to
scream and
cry
before we can
talk.

When someone
inevitably
hurts you,
don't withhold
forgiveness
from them –

it's more healing
for you
than it is
for them.

Sometimes you
have to
leave home
in order to
find it.

Even if
you can
only help
one person –

help that one.

As the
Earth
holds you,
embrace her back –
in love,
in care,
in the
highest regard.
Our shared
home
needs our
help
in order to
continue
holding us.

Hitting
obstacles
does not mean
you are
failing.
After all –
hitting turbulence
does not mean
the plane is
crashing.

There are
countless reasons to
climb mountains and
to fly on airplanes,
but once you've
seen the
colors of the sunset
from above the
cloud line,
you'll never want
your feet on the
ground
again.

In a digital
world, get in
touch with
real,
tangible things –
dust off
photo
albums,
listen to
music on
vinyl,
watch old
family films.

Touch the
past
with your
fingertips.

Fall in
love with
rainy days –
find the
somber beauty in the
petrichor,
the romance in the
hush
covering the
earth.

Find your
gloomy, cozy music
and a
cup of tea
to pair with it,
and you'll
find yourself looking
forward to rainy days,
too.

-rainy days are for death cab for cutie
-also for john mayer

If someone comes to
mind, don't
hesitate to
reach out to
them –

you may
not get
another
chance.

-i should have texted you

Don't let the
prospect of
grief
prevent you from
loving.

Grief hurts.
Oh, how it
hurts.
but love –
oh, love –
there is
nothing
like it in the
whole
universe.

Pretty please –

never,
ever,
ever,
let the
chains of
addiction
ensnare you,
precious one.

Please don't
betray
yourself
or your
family
that way.

-i beg of you

You never
know who will
still be
in your
life
ten years
from now.

Don't count
anybody
out.

-i'm glad you're (still) here

It's not
always
going to be
easy,

but, I
promise,

it won't
always
be this
hard.

Keep your
standards
high
in regard to
how others should
treat you.

Keep them
high
in regard to
how you
treat others,
too.

It is
impossible
to please
everyone.
Save your
efforts
for the
right
people.

Throw that
soggy tennis ball
over and over
again,
even when you're
over it.

A time will come
when you'll
wish you had
someone to
throw it for.

-pets are family, too

Take too
many
photographs –
one day,
they'll be
the only
memories
you have
left.

There is
wisdom
all around you
if you are
willing to
ask,
listen,
and perhaps
most importantly,
discern.

If someone is only
in your life
for a
season,
that's okay.

You can still
cheer them on
from afar.

Sometimes love
requires
letting go.

Cling to the
unabashed,
goblin-like
love of
summer play
for as long as
possible –

cover yourself in
sweat and
dandelions and
grass stains and
bruises and
sunscreen and

joy.

Let your
heart
feel what it
needs to
in order to
heal,
but remember –

the hurt
won't last
forever.

-this too shall pass

Reading
gives you the
chance to
explore
more than just
one world.

Be skeptical of
your own
heart
and in tune with
your own
gut.

Your feelings can
lie to you,
but your
intuition
can guide you.

You can't
change it

but

you can
grow from it.

Their intentions
won't always be
pure –

but yours
can be.

There will
always
be people
who try to
steal
your joy.

Don't
let them.

Snuggle in
on those
peaceful, rainy
weekend mornings,
when the
world still feels
serene.

Savor moments
that calm your
soul.

Even if
everyone
is rooting
against you –

persist.

It is
not
your fault you are
being targeted
by Pain
so young,
sweet child.

I wish you
never had to
know the
sting of
his attacks,
but especially
not
so soon.

-stay away from her

Step into someone
else's
experience
before you
criticize
their choices.

-you really don't know

Your voice
has far more
impact
than you will
realize
until you
use it.

-speak up
-speak out

Take the
time, and
brave the
mess –

it's
worth it to
play
in the
puddles.

Never underestimate
the power
of an
invitation.

-love your neighbor

Treasure those
who give you their
best
even when you are
at your
worst.

Then,
take turns.

It will be
different
from what you
expect it to be

and that's good

because it will be
better
than you
expect
it to
be.

I always loved
chasing fireflies those
summer nights of my childhood,
but now I feel
as though I am
the firefly
on the inside of
the jar –
displaced in a
familiar yet
foreign
environment,
given barely enough
to
survive,
completely out of my
element,
feeling pressured to
perform
with every
tap-tap-tap
on the side of the
glass.

What I wouldn't
give to be
back outside on a
warm June evening
without a
care in the
world but

searching for
the next
yellow
glow.

Check in on
your friends.

Trust your
gut
if you feel
that something
isn't
right.

Risk being
wrong and
overbearing
rather than
right and
regretful.

There will be
times
when you'll
wish
they were
far away,

but there
will
come a day
when you'll
wish
they were
within
arm's reach.

-family

I once received
a compliment
that transformed the
way I carry
myself:

You wear
gratitude
beautifully.

I'll tell you a
secret –

you can,
too.

Anyone
can shell out
a grand gesture
with minimal
effort.

Stand by the
one who
accompanies you
through the
mundane,
through the
weeknights of
leftovers and
reruns.

Stand by the
one who
stays with you
through the
pain, the
grief, the
sorrows
of life.

Stand by the
one who
encourages you,
uplifts you,
empowers you
consistently.

Stand by the
one whose
grand gesture
is themself.

Commune with
creation –

the very
soil
you stand on
is sacred.

You haven't even
dreamed your
biggest
dream yet.

-surprise yourself

Look,
listen, and
learn from the
loved ones
all around you.

There is a
lifetime of
lessons to
learn,
wisdom to
absorb, and
love to share.

-happy 35th anniversary, mom and dad

Always be
willing to
extend
grace
to others.

Never forget –
sometimes
you need
others
to extend it
to you,
too.

-stay humble

Many people
will try to
guide you,
but your
decisions are
ultimately
yours
to make.

Choose
wisely.

Reserve
your precious
energy
for the people
who are
worthy
of it.

-not everyone is

Use the
words of your
naysayers
as your
biggest
motivation –

then thank them
in a witty way
from the
top of the
hill you've
climbed.

-have i been listening to too much taylor swift?

The pain you
feel is valid and
real, but honey,
I promise you,
that teenage boy
is not your
future husband.

It's going to
be okay.

-why did i waste so many tears on them?

God loves you,
and all of His
creatures, too.

Be kind
to them.

They were here
first.

-"sheila the turtle is my friend."

Knowing the
difference between
This can be ignored
and
This is a red flag
is
critical.

Intentions
can be
difficult to
discern.

-stay vigilant

You keep
looking around for
a miracle
without even realizing
that you
are one.

Sometimes you
can't give a
reason why...

and *that's*
why.

Being a
giver
is a
rare gift
in and of
itself,

but –

never let
others take
all of you
from yourself.

Pain can both
torture and
teach,
scar and
sow,
eviscerate and
enlighten.

After the
harm comes
healing.

How could I
understand
how much I would
long for
warm summer
midnights
sitting in bed
with the windows open,
the world silent
save for the
soft chirps of
crickets,
as I devour
one of many
chosen summer
books,
no worries
other than
repeating the
routine again
tomorrow?

How could I
have known
even that
had an
expiration date?

-literature girl summer

Beware those
who relish the
idea of
"the chase,"
those who
allow their prey
just far enough to be
"hard to get,"
but still within
their sights.

Be on your
guard for the
expert marksman –
hunters who
simply want
another
gruesome trophy
and bragging rights
from winning
another
tantalizing,
flirtatious
game.

-1 in 4

Don't you
dare
underestimate
the
intuition
of a
child.

You, dear one,
deserve so
much more
than to
simply be
tolerated.

Be seen
and
be heard.

Challenge
anyone
who claims
that you do
not deserve
a seat at
their table.

-auntie dares you

Be the friend
who faithfully
defends
their friends.

-i'd do anything for you

Learn to be
content with
life in the
gray –

happiness and pain,
joy and grief,
hope and fear,
love and anger,
clarity and confusion –

existence
is rarely
anything
other than
paradox.

Never
take
time with your
friends
for granted.

You may
think
life will
stay like this
forever,
but the
time together will
become shorter, the
miles between will
expand, and the
weight of life will
grow heavier.

But –
if you put in
the work,
the love
will stay like this
forever.

There will be
moments
when the
correct response
is to
propose a
solution.

There will be
other moments
when the
correct response
is simply
compassion.

Know your
audience.

You are not
required
to dig up the
past
for the sake of
closure –

yours or
anyone else's.

-let it rest

Life
certainly is a
grand
adventure,
but, my darling,
so are
you.

-i love having fun with you

The labor of
love that is
justice
for all
isn't over
yet.

The baton
is being
passed on to
you.

Will you take it?

-juneteenth

Your best
efforts
with people
won't always be
reciprocated.

Try anyway,
then move
on.

Always try to
include
others.

Life is
more fun with
diversity.

I thought I
knew what
life on standby
meant, until I
flew on standby.

Now I
understand
the anxiety
of anticipation,
of not knowing
if you are
getting on the
flight.
Now I
Understand
what this means
outside the
airport, too.

But I made an
assumption
without the
lived experience
to back it up.

In other words –
I took the
fast route
to making myself look
foolish.

God didn't
have to make
creatures as
beautiful and
gentle as
fireflies, but
He did.

He didn't
have to make
you and me,
either.

But He did.

Don't wait
for a
tragedy
to
realize that
your time is
not
infinite.

Say
the things
you need to
say.
Do
the things
you want to
do.

Live your
life
while you
have the
time
to live it.

-"like the world is going to end," ben rector

Don't be
afraid
to soar
high.

People will
warn you to
stay far
away from the
sun, for
fear of
scorching
their wings.

But you,
precious one,
are a
phoenix –
if your
wings burn,
you will
rise
from the
ashes and
fly
again.

Don't let those with
unreachable standards
make you
doubt
yourself.

They are probably
doubting themselves
enough
anyways.

Just because you've
moved on
doesn't mean
you have
forgotten
how you felt.

You can be
over it
and still feel the
sting
like it
just happened.

-"whatsername," green day

All you can do is
your best.

Some will try to
help you get there.
Some will try to
tell you that it's
not enough.
And some will try to
stop you.

But all you can
control is
you.

Growing older
is not the
same as
growing up.

Some people
will never
learn the
difference
or experience
both.

At the
end of it all,
you won't regret
the meetings you
missed, or the
vacation days you used.
You'll regret
the chances you
didn't take,
the memories you
didn't make,
and the time
you let slip
away.

-live it well

Get to know
your neighbors
in every stage
of life –

the people who
live next door,
the people whose
lockers are on
either side,
the people in the
dorm across the hall,
the person in the
adjacent cubicle.

These are all
people that God
has put in
your path
whom you can
bless.

Treasure the
little things.
One day, you'll see
they were
big things
all along.

I'm so glad
I know you
is one of the
kindest things
you can tell
someone.

It is also
one of the
kindest things
to be told.

Things that are
okay to say:

I wasn't done
talking.

I don't think
that's funny.

Thank you, but
I'm not looking for
suggestions.

No.

Practice saying them.

What I wouldn't
give for the
world to be as
simple as it
appears in your
eyes.

The moment you
realize
you aren't
bound to the
standards of
society...

I don't think
I've ever
felt a
feeling
quite as
liberating.

Make sure that
your table
remains a
welcoming
refuge
and not an
exclusionary
social club.

Be suspicious
of those who
explain away
or
make excuses
instead of
apologizing.

Being assertive
is not the
same thing as
being rude.

Learn this
before others
assume
you are a
doormat.

Society constantly
pits women
against one another,
but one place they
have failed to
do so is the
public restroom.
Here's how I
know:

Ask anyone
in there for a
tampon, and,
if she is able,
she will give you one,
no hesitation.

Every woman
has asked for
and given assistance
to total strangers
without shame or
judgment.

Our instincts make us
so much more
interdependent
than others would
have you
believe.

-sisterhood

It is
time to
stop
pretending
that our
bodies
are gross.

It is
not
shameful
to have
or talk about
periods.

-sisterhood, part two

People will
remember
how you
made them
feel.

Be mindful
of the
legacy
that you
leave behind.

There will
always be
more to add
to your
to-do list.
You'll never feel
"done."
Don't let that
keep you from
the things in
life that
really matter.

You have a
voice.
You are
allowed to
use it.
Be loud and
take up
space.

I wish I
hadn't
waited
so long
to find my
Big Girl
Voice.

Don't let the
risk of
getting hurt
keep you from
letting people
in.
There will be
some who
do hurt you, but
there will be
more who
prove that
they were
worth
the risk.

There will
always be
willing contributors
to the
world's chaos.

You do not
have to be
one of them.

Your time with
loved ones is
limited,
and doesn't
come with an
expiration date.

Take advantage
of the
time you are
granted.

-it's never enough

Stop
apologizing
for doing
what's right
for you.

Sometimes mean kids
turn into
mean adults.
Bullies don't
disappear
once you
graduate.

Learn to
deal with them
without
becoming one.

Stand up
for yourself
without
stooping to
their level.

You'll never
fly
if you don't
leave
the nest.

-it's worth the leap

When you have
nothing
left to give,
give it to
God.

-surrender

Love the people
in your
life
out loud.

-don't hold back

When
thinking things over,
remember –
there is a
big difference
between
marinating
and
festering.

Nothing
is ever
accomplished
alone.

We need
each other.

If you wait
until you
feel ready –
you'll
never
do it.

All my life,
I've been
surprised
by how much
my
capacity to
love
has grown.
Just when I
think my
heart has
reached its
limit, it expands.

You will
always
have more
love
to give.

Hand in hand,
let's brave this
path together –
I'll lead with the
wisdom from
past treks, and
you'll follow
with the
joy and vigor
of a new
adventure.

-wisdom and youth

When my soul
returns to
the heavens,
and my
body to the
earth –
promise me
that you
won't let my
words fade
into oblivion.

You are going to
accomplish
amazing things.
I can't wait
to see you
shine.

Everyone
deserves a
safe space.

I promise
to be
yours.

-with you till the end of the line

Acknowledgments

I have an ever growing list of special people to thank; for that alone, I am so grateful!

Lex – I am so thankful to have such an encouraging and empowering husband. You didn't doubt my ability to publish another book four months after my first; instead, you asked what my vision for the cover was and how you could help. You're my best friend, and the most wonderful support system I could ever ask for. I'm so blessed to have you (and Rocket) by my side.

Melanie – as promised, "you are the wind beneath my wings." I hit the jackpot in the sister lottery. Thank you for always cheering me on, and for being an advanced reader. Your feedback always means the world, but it certainly meant a lot on this one, since the dedication involves your children! I love being their Auntie Lindsay more than anything, and seeing you being a super mom is so inspiring. You're an absolute rockstar, and they are so blessed to have you.

Mom and Dad – you've always believed in what I could accomplish, even when I've doubted myself. Thank you for your endless support. I love you both so much.

Grandma Sharon – seeing your copy of *Captive* already so beaten up is pretty much the only validation I will ever need as an author. Thank you for being my biggest fan and cheerleader, and my best friend. I love you so much.

I could write an entire book just of people that I could thank for supporting me on this journey! But know that I love you all, and thank you so much for reading.

Thank You

I asked for inspiration and life lessons, and I received so much beautiful wisdom from many amazing people. Thank you, from the bottom of my heart.

Lindsay Wilhoft
Alison Lawrence
Emily Kasai
Jordan Fallert
Jorie Secker
Maren Spaulding
Michael Dufresne III
Kelly Dufresne
Jess Parker
Brandy Buckholt
Jen Watson
Kristen Peters
Heather Boyd
Julie Thomas
Kim Becker
Pam Matyka
Stephen Sticklen
Chelsey Walker
Kristin Giolas
Kris Hayden

About the Author

Lindsay Gordon is a youth pastor, singer, dog mom, and cancer survivor. After growing up in Chicagoland with a love of reading and writing, she received her Bachelor's degree in English Education from Olivet Nazarene University. Lindsay is now pursuing her Master of Divinity degree at Princeton Theological Seminary. When she is not writing, you can find her in the forest or the mountains with her husband, Lex, and her dog, Rocket. As an extrovert, Lindsay loves connecting with different people. You can find her and her upcoming work on Instagram @linesbylinds, or at linesbylinds.com.

MORE TITLES BY LINDSAY GORDON

CAPTIVE: A COLLECTION OF POEMS

www.ingramcontent.com/pod-product-compliance
Ingram Content Group UK Ltd.
Pitfield, Milton Keynes, MK11 3LW, UK
UKHW022002190726
13853UKWH00004B/1693